A course for young beginners learning to play alto saxophone

Illustrations by Melody-Anne Lee

kevin mayhew

The *Super Sax* series will take you from your very first lesson to around Grade 4 level in Book 3.
There are many interesting pieces, including some for ensemble playing.
There are also exercises to improve technique, listening games and puzzles.
Have fun!

Heather Hammond

Key to symbols

CD track.

Exercises that will help you play rhythmically.

Exercises that will help you listen carefully.

Exercises that will help you to get a good sound and help your breath control.

Know the notes

Exercise patterns for getting to know the notes.

OCTAVE HOPS

Exercise patterns for getting a good sound between notes.

kevin mayhew

First published in Great Britain in 2012 by Kevin Mayhew Ltd
Buxhall, Stowmarket, Suffolk IP14 3BW
Tel: +44 (0) 1449 737978
Fax: +44 (0) 1449 737834
E-mail: info@kevinmayhew.com

www.kevinmayhew.com

The publishers wish to thank all those who have given their permission to reproduce copyright material in this publication.

Every effort has been made to trace the owners of copyright material and we hope that no copyright has been infringed. Pardon is sought and apology made if the contrary be the case, and a correction will be made in any reprint of this book.

9 8 7 6 5 4 3 2 1 0

ISBN 978 1 84867 574 2
ISMN M 57042 191 6
Catalogue No. 3612489

Music Editor: Donald Thomson
Illustration and design: Melody-Anne Lee

Printed and bound in Great Britain

Contents

Things you need to know

Before you start playing the music in this book you'll need to check that you know the following information from Book 1.

Notes you learnt from *Super Sax* Book 1

Note	Octave key	L1	L2	L3	R1	R2	R3
Low E		●	●	●	●	●	○
F		●	●	●	●	○	○
F♯		●	●	●	○	●	○
G		●	●	●	○	○	○
A		●	●	○	○	○	○
B♭		●	●	○	○	○	○
B		●	○	○	○	○	○
C		○	●	○	○	○	○
C♯		○	○	○	○	○	○
D	●	●	●	●	●	●	●
High E	●	●	●	●	●	●	○

Note values

𝅝	Semibreve	Worth 4 beats
𝅗𝅥.	Dotted minim	Worth 3 beats
𝅗𝅥	Minim	Worth 2 beats
♩	Crotchet	Worth 1 beat
♪	Quaver	Worth $^1/_2$ beat
♫	2 Quavers	Together worth 1 beat

Rest values

	Semibreve	Be silent for 4 beats. This sign can also be used to indicate silence for a whole bar (no matter how many beats there are in the bar).
	Minim	Be silent for 2 beats.
𝄽	Crotchet	Be silent for 1 beat.

Dynamics

Always add the dynamics to make your playing interesting.

f	or forte means loud.
mf	or mezzo forte means quite loud.
mp	or mezzo piano means quite soft.
p	or piano means soft.
	or crescendo means gradually get louder.
	or diminuendo means gradually get softer.

Signs

♯	Sharp	Makes the note slightly higher than it usually is.
♭	Flat	Makes the note slightly lower than it usually is.
♮	Natural	Cancels out sharps and flats and means that you just play the normal note.
	Accidentals	An accidental (sharp, flat or natural sign that appears beside a note) affects the other notes of that pitch for the rest of the bar in which it appears, e.g. in the first tune 'Billy boy blue' the fourth note of bar 11 is C natural (not C sharp).

SET 1

Here's a tune using all of the notes that you learnt in Book 1.

Billy boy blue

TRACK 1 COMPLETE
TRACK 2 BACKING

Bluesy

2nd time to Coda

Boogie

D.S. al Coda *CODA*

rall.

Reminders

Staccato A dot either below or above a note makes it short and crisp.

Legato The curved sign is called a slur and you should play the notes smoothly (just tongue the first note then move smoothly onto the next notes all in the same breath).

Each of the notes that are not marked with a slur or a staccato dot should be tongued (try to leave the smallest gap possible between the sounds).

Accent Play the note with extra force.

Ties If both notes are the same letter name you can add the two note values together and just play one note.

Here's a piece for you to practise playing staccato, legato and accented notes.
(Don't forget to make it interesting by adding the dynamics too.)

Time to learn a new rhythm

Dotted Notes A dot after a note makes it last longer. It makes the note half as long again.

𝅗𝅥. We already know that a dotted minim is worth 3 beats in total. The note itself is worth 2 beats and the dot is worth 1 beat (half of the note's value).

♩. A dotted crotchet is worth 1 $^{1}/_{2}$ beats (1 beat for the note and half a beat for the dot).

First clap this

Now tie the first 2 notes of each bar

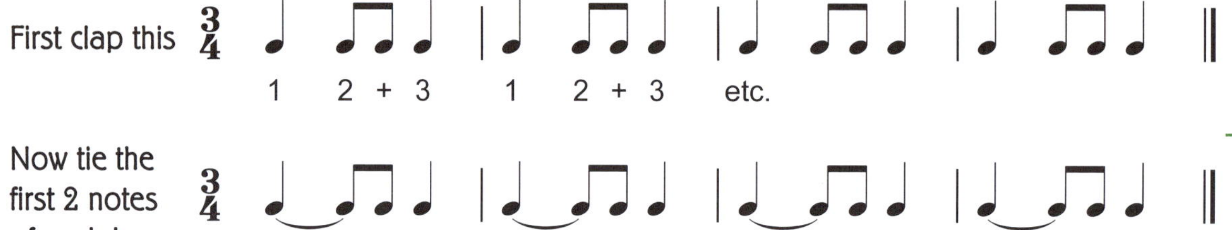

The same rhythm can now be written with the dotted crotchet note instead of the tied crotchet and quaver like this

1 (2) + 3 1 (2) + 3 etc.

These both sound the same

Practise clapping each of these rhythms four times.
Then clap the whole thing through twice with the CD accompaniment.

rit. or **ritenuto** Held back (suddenly slower). This is slightly different to **rall.** or **rallentando** which means becoming gradually slower.

For Lily

Girl in the corner

TRACK 6 COMPLETE
TRACK 7 BACKING

Lively jazz waltz

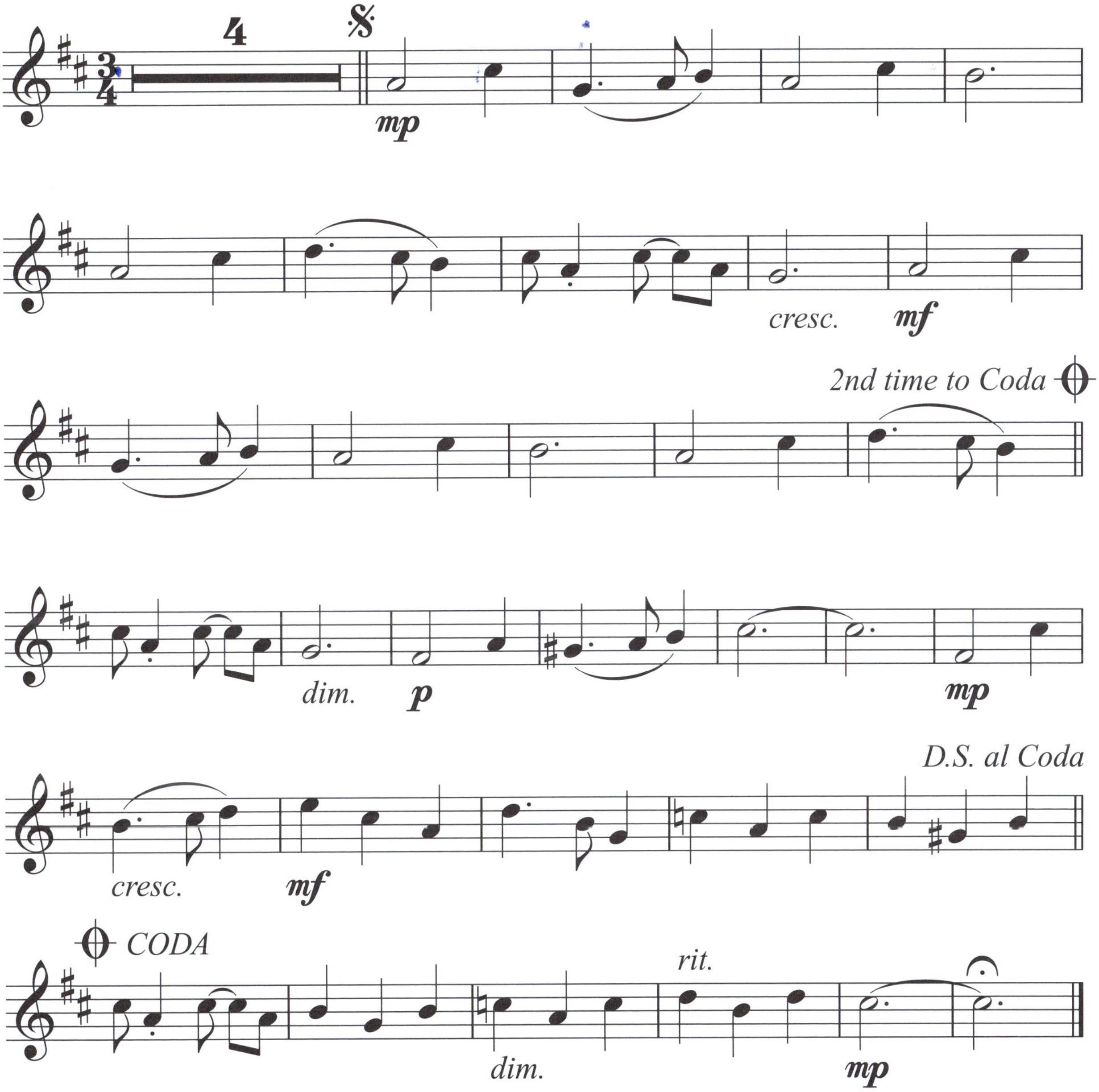

4
mp
cresc.
mf
2nd time to Coda
dim.
p
mp
D.S. al Coda
cresc.
mf
CODA
rit.
dim.
mp

Listening game 1

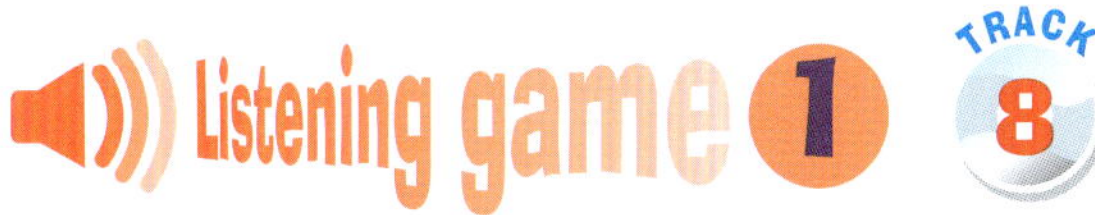

TRACK 8

Using the notes A, B, C♯, and D listen to the CD and try to copy the tunes like an echo.

There are some dotted rhythms included too – see if you can spot which ones they are. There are 3 beats in each bar.

Now try these pieces from
Super Sax Repertoire Book 2

Lillibullero p.7
London Bridge p.8

Heather Hammond's
Super
Sax
Repertoire
A course for young beginners
Book 2

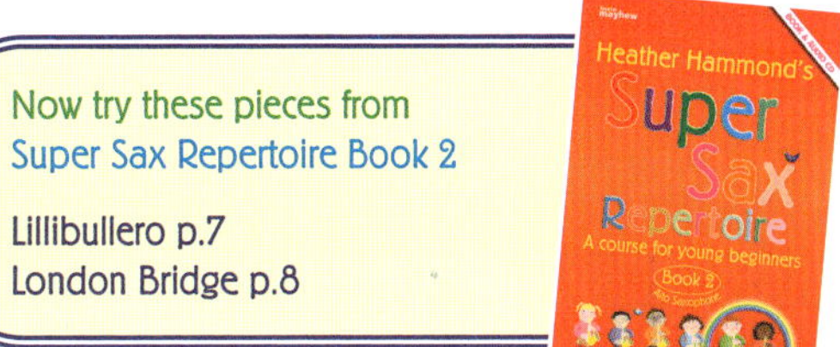

Puzzle it out

Name each of the notes and say how many beats each one is worth.
The first one has been done for you.

Play these well-known tunes. Write in the titles if you know them.

Title: ....

Can you continue?

Title: ....

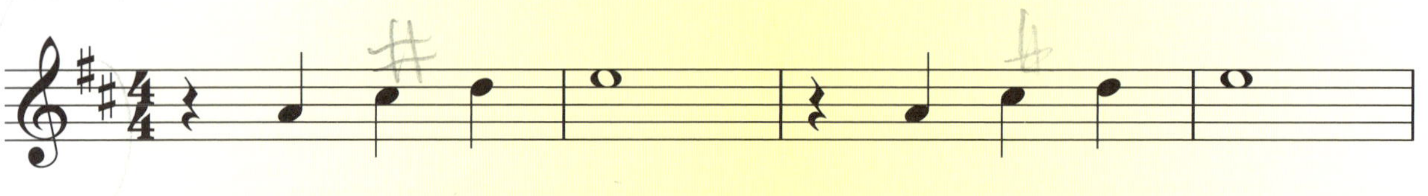

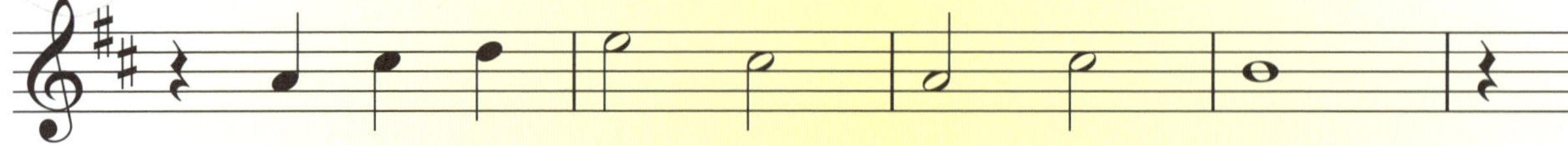

What happens next?

Stems up or down

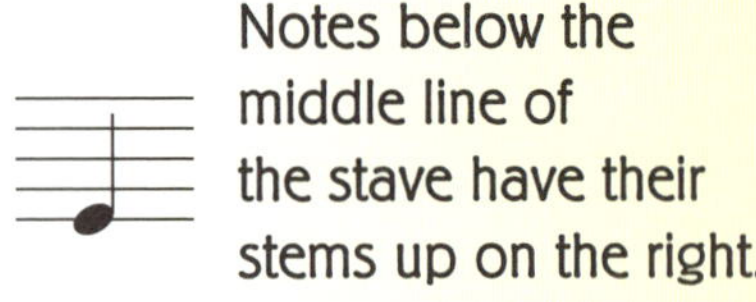

Notes below the middle line of the stave have their stems up on the right.

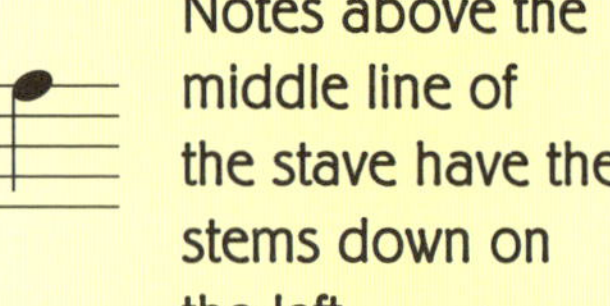

Notes above the middle line of the stave have their stems down on the left.

Notes on the middle line can have their stems either way.

Add stems to these notes

SET 2 The Octave Key

In Book 1 we learnt that to play the notes high D and high E, we need to use the octave key on the back of the saxophone.

Musicians sometimes abbreviate the word octave and write instead: 8ve

When you play the low D followed by the high D (or low E followed by the high E) the only finger movement you need to make is to roll your thumb onto the octave key whilst keeping contact with the thumb rest.
You will need to provide more air for the higher notes (but remember not to bite the reed).

OCTAVE HOPS

Practise each of these patterns twice.
Try to move between the notes as smoothly as possible and get the best sound you can on both the low and high notes.

$\frac{4}{4}$ can also be shown as **C** in the time signature. It means Common time.

The next tune contains some octave leaps between high E and low E:

Medieval minstrels

Now try these pieces from
Super Sax Repertoire Book 2

Westward Waltz p.10
Turbo charged p.12

Remember, it's best to practise for a short while every day rather than doing a great big practice every now and again.

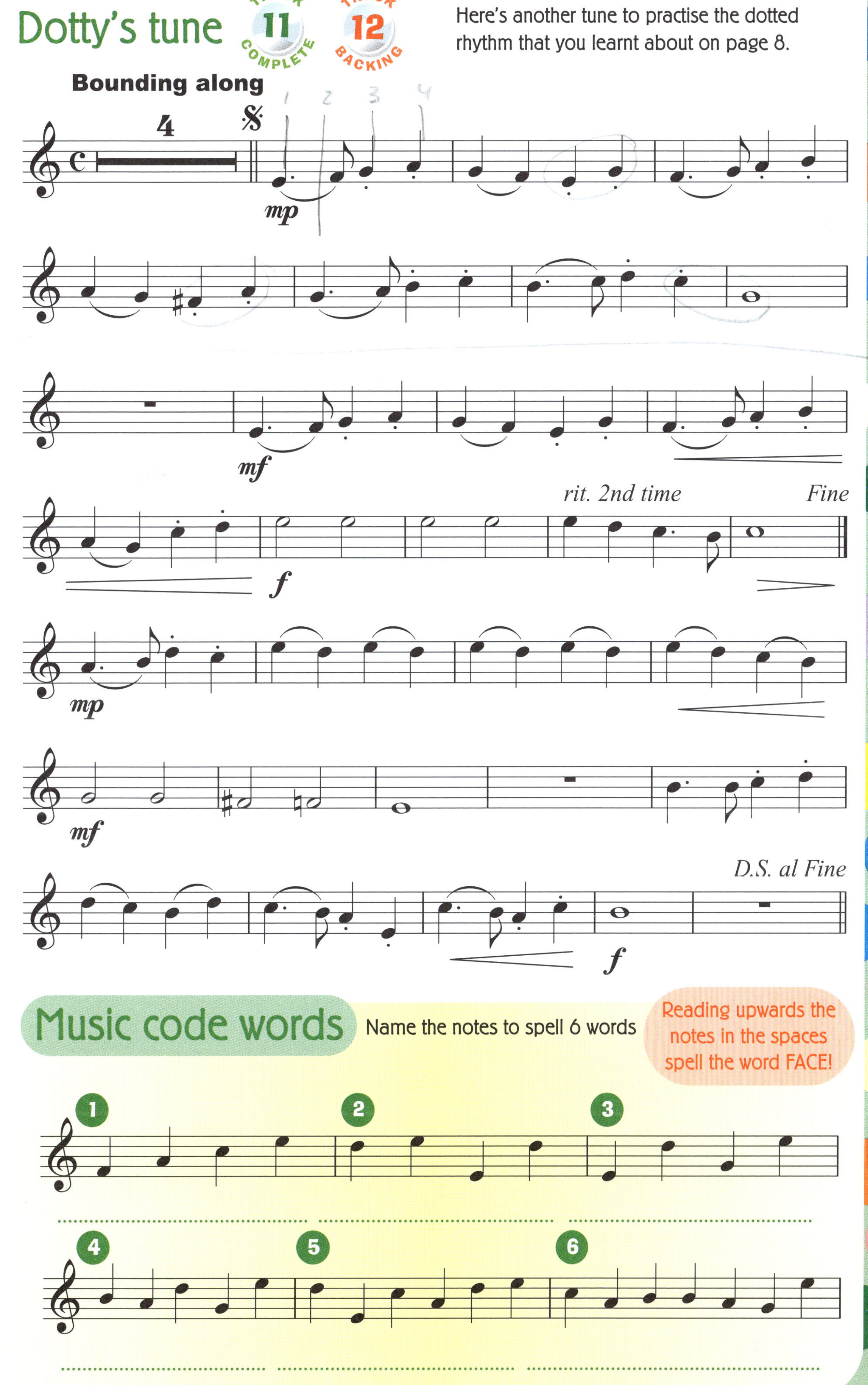
Dotty's tune
TRACK 11 COMPLETE
TRACK 12 BACKING
Here's another tune to practise the dotted rhythm that you learnt about on page 8.
Bounding along
4
mp
mf
rit. 2nd time
Fine
f
mp
mf
D.S. al Fine
f
Music code words
Name the notes to spell 6 words
Reading upwards the notes in the spaces spell the word FACE!
1
2
3
4
5
6

SET 3 A new note – high F

This is what high F looks like on the stave

Remember the fingering is just the same as the low F with the addition of the octave key.

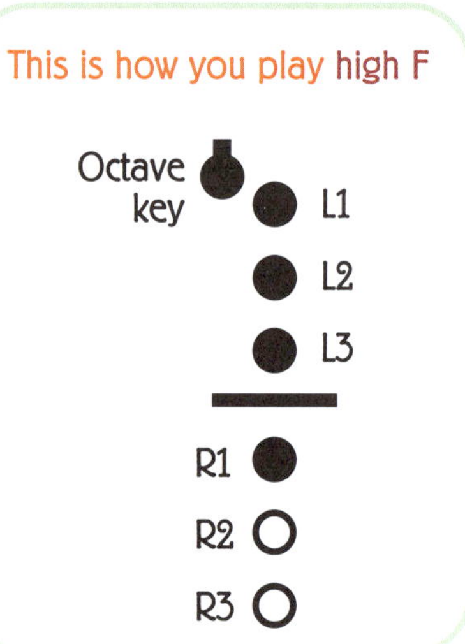

Know the notes

Practise each of these patterns four times.

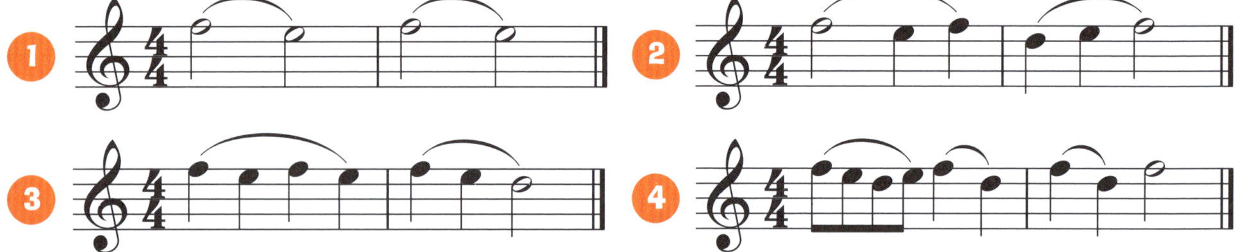

Long note practice 1

TRACK 13

Long note practice is a great way of warming up when you first pick up your sax. Remember to listen carefully and always try to get the best sound possible.

F major scale

Tongue each note. Remember to leave just a small gap between each sound.

The scale of F major uses all of the notes in the key of F major. Musicians practise scales to become familiar with note patterns that are likely to appear in pieces of music.

When you've learnt a particular scale try to keep playing it regularly and learn it from memory if possible. You'll need to play scales if you decide to take a saxophone examination in the future!

After darkness

TRACK 14 COMPLETE

TRACK 15 BACKING

With mystery

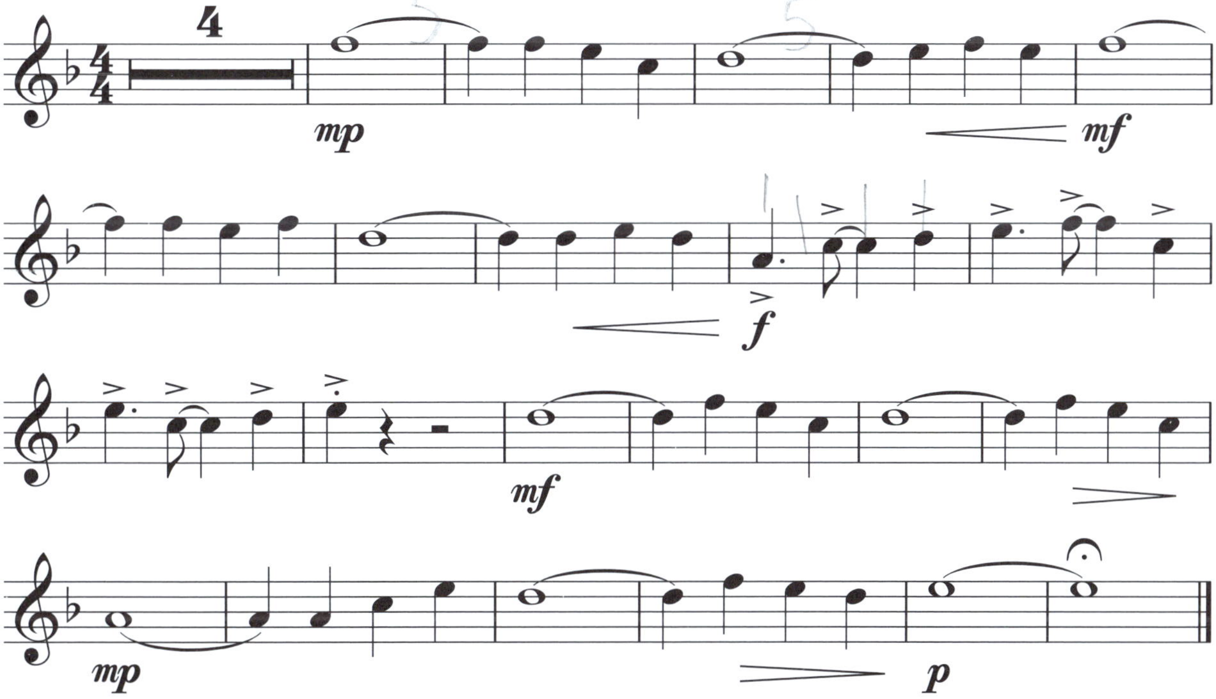

4

mp *mf*

f

mf

mp *p*

The position of the mouthpiece on the crook affects the tuning. If you need to play slightly lower in pitch pull the mouthpiece off the crook a little. If you need to be higher in pitch, push the mouthpiece further on. You will probably only need to adjust the pitch very slightly.

Another note – high F sharp

This is what high F sharp (F♯) looks like on the stave

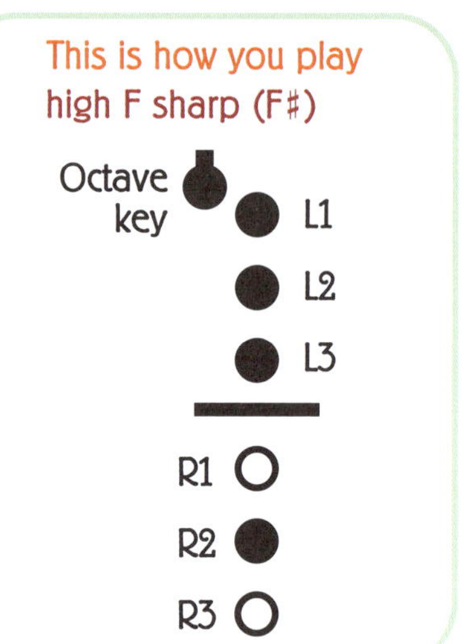

Know the notes

Practise each of these patterns four times.

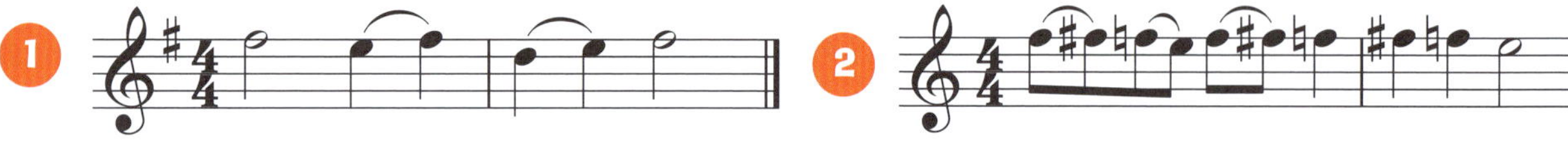

OCTAVE HOPS AGAIN

Try these tricky octave-hop exercises.
Beware – play slowly to start with, they're not easy.

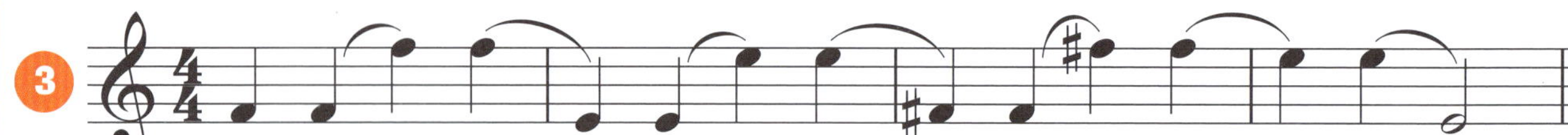

. . . a really hard challenge

Sam's samba

Allegro

mf

f

p cresc.

f

rall.

p cresc.

f

Now try this piece from Super Sax Repertoire Book 2 The Can-Can p.13

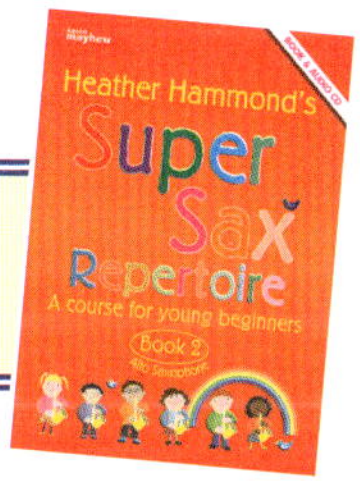

Road signs quiz

Whilst travelling along you meet the following road signs. Can you join each sign to its meaning? (use the rhythms to help you)

CROSSROADS NO CYCLING ROUNDABOUT SLIPPERY ROAD
ONE WAY TRAFFIC NO OVERTAKING MINI-ROUNDABOUT
TRAFFIC QUEUES LIKELY NO TOWED CARAVANS
BEND TO THE RIGHT COMING UP

SET 4 Here's – high G and high A

This is what high G looks like on the stave

This is how you play high G

Octave key ● L1 ● L2 ● L3 ●

R1 ○ R2 ○ R3 ○

G major scale

Always check the key signature before you start to play.

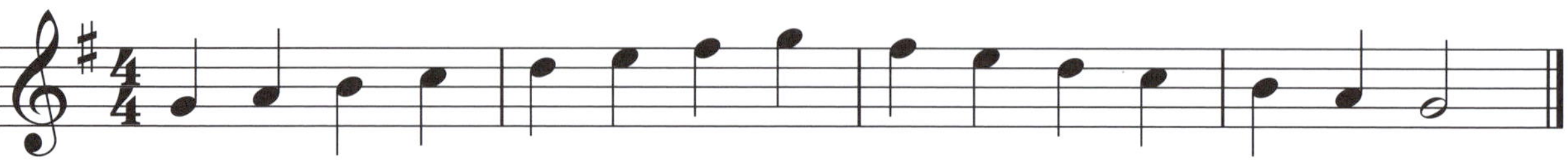

This is what high A looks like on the stave

This is how you play high A

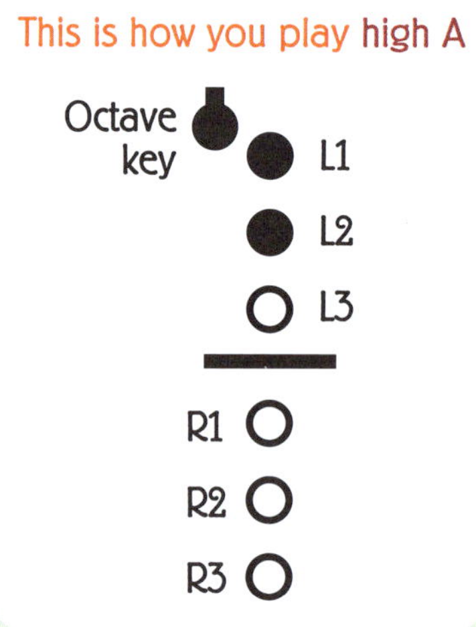

Again these two new notes are just the same as the lower versions with the addition of the octave key.

When you run out of lines on the stave because you want to go even higher, you can just add extra lines to put the high notes on. These are called leger lines.

Know the notes

Practise each of these patterns four times.

fortissimo is the Italian word for very loud, it is written in the music as *ff*.
pianissimo is the Italian word for very soft and it will say *pp* on your music.
𝄾 This is a quaver rest. You have to be silent for half a beat.

High above the clouds

TRACK 18 COMPLETE
TRACK 19 BACKING

RHYTHM WORKOUT 2

TRACK 5

Practise clapping each of these rhythms four times with a friend or your teacher, then swap parts. Beware, they're quite tricky! When you've mastered them all try clapping the whole thing through twice with the CD accompaniment.

Another fingering for B flat

In Book 1 we learnt that B flat could be produced by using the right hand side key (see page 4 if you need to revise that fingering). However, there is another way of playing B flat that many sax players prefer.

Position your left hand forefinger so that it's touching both the normal B key as well the bis key. You don't need to fully cover either of the two keys – your finger will be between the two.

You can use the bis key for all B flats unless there's a B natural either just before or just after it.

Use the exercises to practise using the B flat played with the bis key.

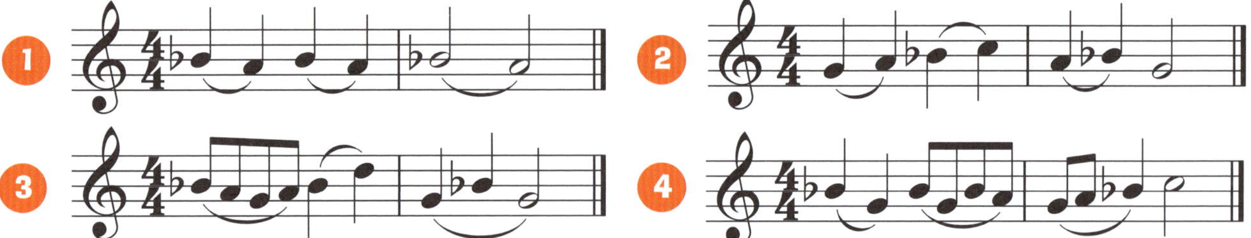

Also try playing the scale of F major (see page 15) using the bis key for B♭.

A short line above or below a note tells you to stress the note slightly (tenuto). It's not as strong as an accent though.

più means more
mosso means movement

So from bar 19 in the next piece you need to go faster. Remember to go back to the original speed again (a tempo) when you return to the 𝄋 sign.

Snow bird's journey

TRACK 20 COMPLETE

TRACK 21 BACKING

Use the bis key for the B flats in this piece.

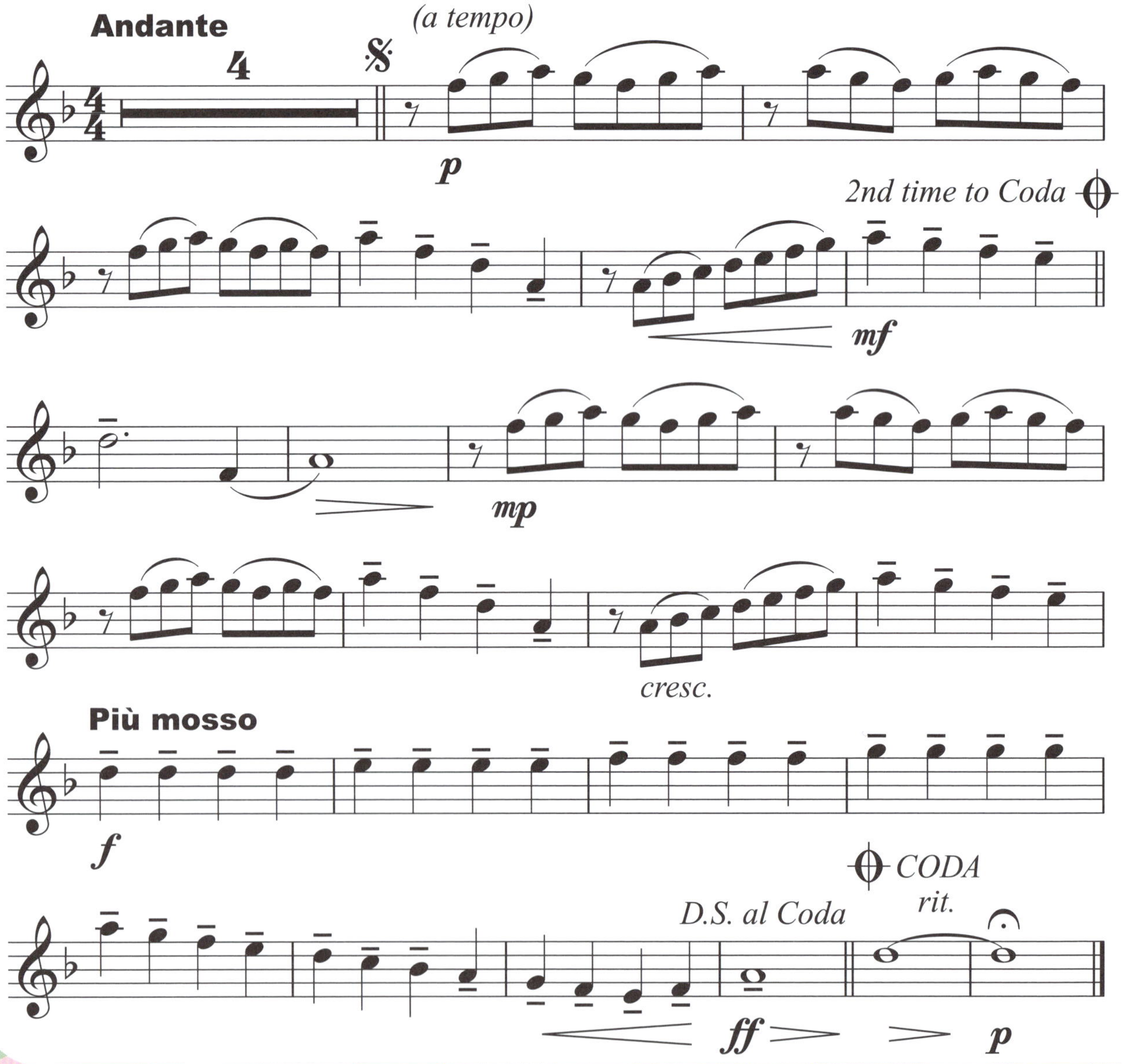

Andante

4

(a tempo)

p

2nd time to Coda 𝄌

mf

mp

cresc.

Più mosso

f

D.S. al Coda

𝄌 *CODA*

rit.

ff

p

If there's a particularly difficult part in the piece you're practising – slowly repeat the tricky notes a few times rather than just playing through the whole piece. It will save you time in the long run.

Wordsearch fun

See if you can you find the hidden musical words.

C	R	N	A	T	U	R	A	L	R
R	O	C	O	D	A	I	Q	U	A
E	J	M	K	N	P	T	U	R	L
S	A	E	M	T	I	E	A	T	L
C	M	V	P	O	S	N	V	O	A
E	F	A	R	S	N	U	E	Z	B
N	L	T	A	C	H	T	R	Z	R
D	A	C	H	A	U	O	I	E	E
O	T	O	S	L	Z	H	D	M	V
L	L	E	G	E	R	L	I	N	E

SHARP
OCTAVE
FLAT
SCALE
NATURAL
MAJOR
TIE
LEGER LINE
CODA
ALLA BREVE
QUAVER
COMMON TIME
CRESCENDO
RITENUTO
MEZZO

Can you remember what they all mean? If not, look back and find out!

Now try these pieces from Super Sax Repertoire Book 2

The ash grove p.14
Ring out the bells on Christmas Morning p.17
She'll be comin' round the mountain p.20
Tim's tango p.22

SET 5 Two new notes – high and low G sharp

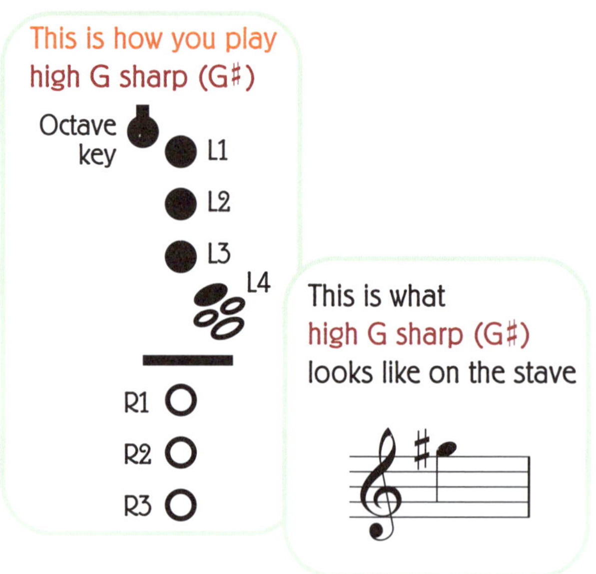

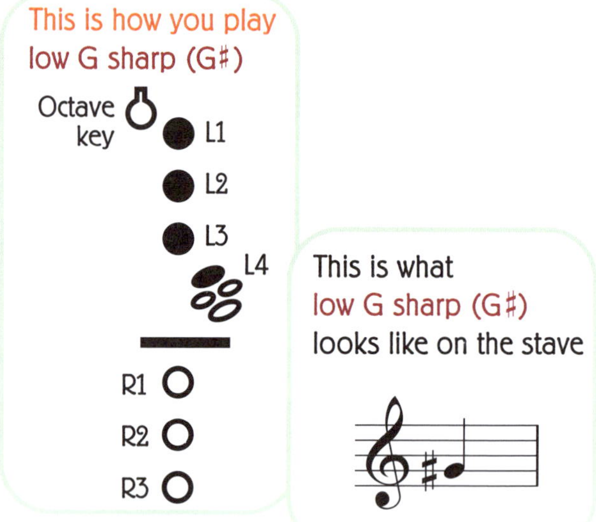

Know the notes

Practise each of these patterns four times.

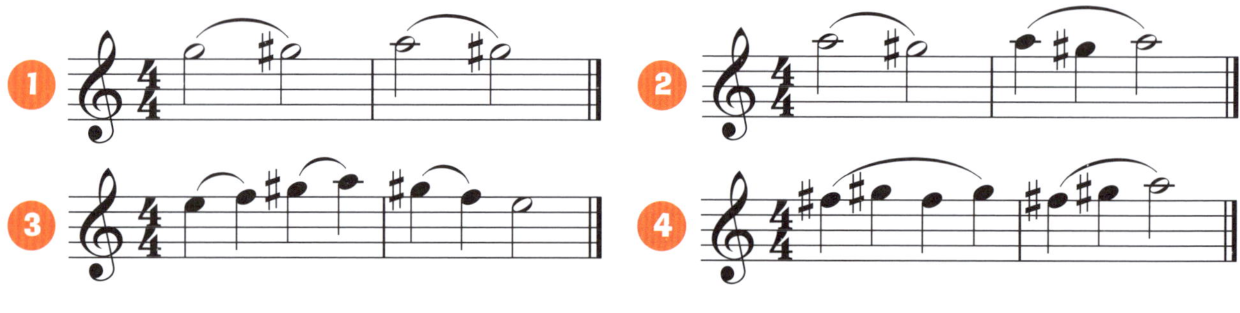

Now play them in the lower register too.

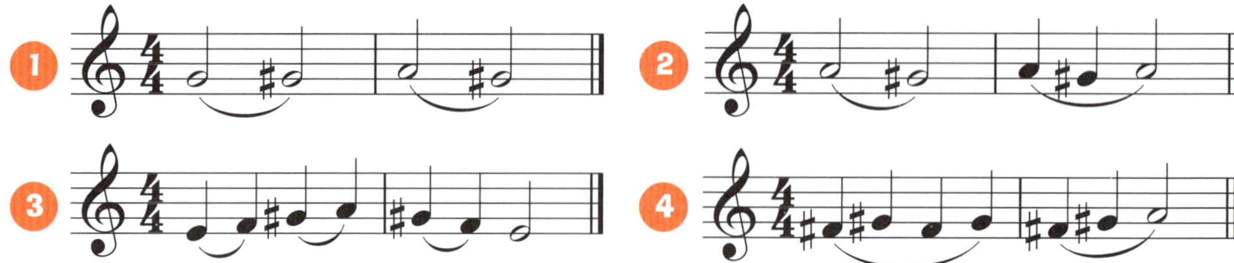

Long note practice 2

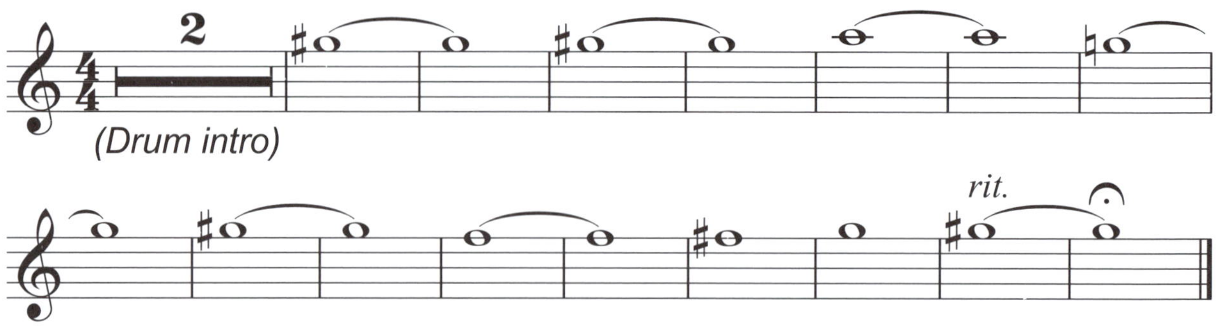

So far you have learnt 2 major scales, F major (p.15) and G major (p.18). Now here's a minor scale:

A harmonic minor scale

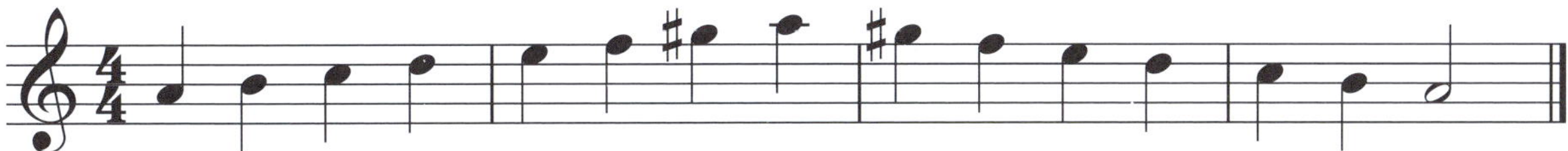

You may think a minor scale sounds quite strange at first, don't worry – you'll get used to the sound of it eventually!

If a composer wishes to write a happy-sounding piece of music they will usually use the notes from a major scale. If notes from minor scales are used the music tends to sound more sad.

Just play the top 5 notes of the A harmonic minor scale.

It may remind you of music that a snake charmer would play.

Use the 5 notes above to compose your own snake charmer tune here:

Snake charmer style

Using the same 5 notes, listen to the CD and try to copy the snake charmer tunes like an echo. The first one starts on high A.

(Don't worry if you don't get them all perfect – they're not easy!)

Remember to check your posture in a mirror – are you still standing/sitting up straight?

$\frac{2}{2}$ This means count 2 minims in every bar. Tip: Just count 4 crotchet beats in each bar when you first start learning tunes in $\frac{2}{2}$ time. It is sometimes referred to as alla breve time and can also be shown as ¢.

Jump

With a lively and jumpy beat

Same note with a different name A flat (A♭)

(A♭ has exactly the same fingering as G♯.)

This is what A flat (A♭) looks like on the stave

A♭ is the note that is slightly lower than A (the distance between normal A and A♭ is called a semitone). G♯ is the note that is slightly higher (a semitone higher) than G. There is only one note between G and A so it means that A flat and G sharp are in fact the same note (it would be a black note on the piano). When a note can be referred to by two different names this is called an enharmonic.

In the next two pieces there are some A♭s and G♯s to watch out for.

Also try using the bis key for B flats (apart from the final one in *Creepy Castle* because it comes after a B natural).

Midnight ramble

Rambling along

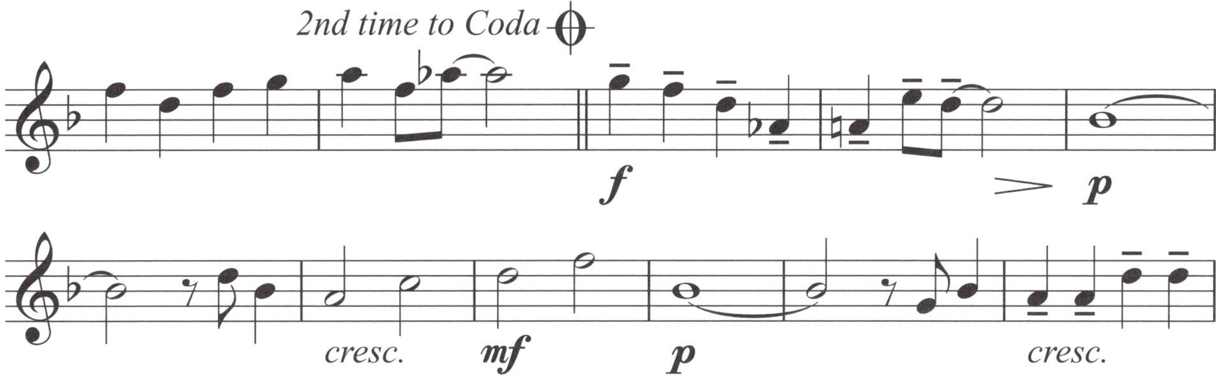

Creepy Castle

Adagio means play slowly.

Adagio *(watch out - ghosts about!)*

Creepy Castle conundrum
The ghosts in Creepy Castle are getting ready to do their midnight haunting. Can you show each of them which window they need to go through to start their spooking?
Alla breve 2/2
Quaver note
Play slowly
Adagio
Common time 4/4
More movement
Octave
Ritenuto
a tempo
Held back (slower at once)
Più mosso
Back to the original speed
Note worth 1 1/2 crotchet beats
Rest worth 1/2 crotchet beat
A♭
Now try these pieces from Super Sax Repertoire Book 2
Sticky toffee sundae p.24, Ballad for Erik p.26, Daisy Bell p.28, Cycling song p.30
Heather Hammond's Super Sax Repertoire
26

SET 6 New quick notes – semiquavers

This is a semiquaver. It is worth ¼ of a beat.

Four of them together are played evenly in the time of one crotchet beat.

Other rhythms that you might come across including semiquavers are

= Each equals 1 beat

Practise clapping each of these rhythms four times. Say the words as you clap – they will help you to get the rhythms correct. Then clap the whole thing through twice with the CD accompaniment.

1. 4/4 Tea, tea, co-ca co-la, tea. Co-ca co-la, cof-fee, milk.

2. 4/4 Co-ca co-la, tea, straw-ber-ry, tea. Straw-ber-ry, co-ca co-la, tea, tea.

3. 4/4 Le-mon-ade, tea. Le-mon-ade, tea. Le-mon-ade, co-ca co-la, cof-fee, tea.

4. 4/4 Wa-ter and tea. Wa-ter and tea. Wa-ter and co-ca co-la, wa-ter and tea.

Always concentrate when you are playing – you will make much faster progress than when you are only half thinking about what you're doing!

Haunted house

Topsy-turvy tango

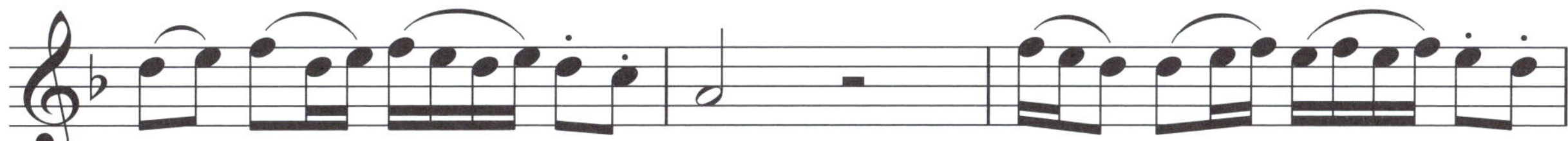

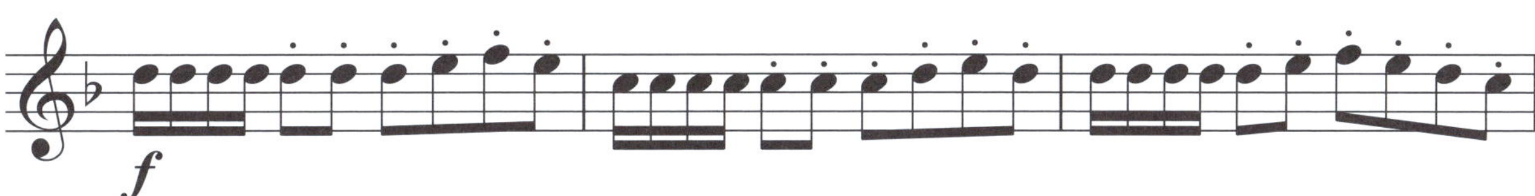

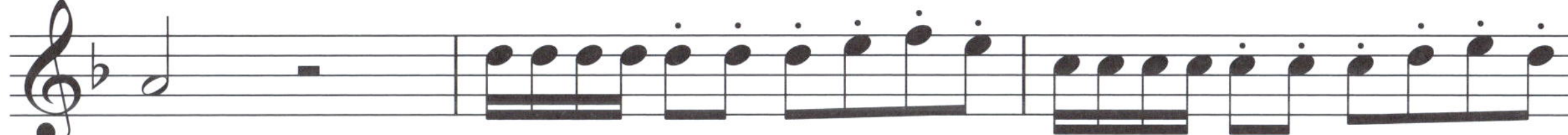

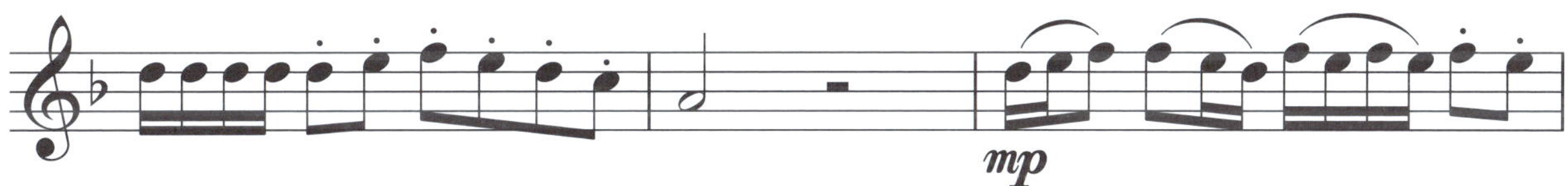

Test your memory

See if you can play the 3 scales that you have learnt from memory

F major scale
G major scale
A minor scale

Remember to wipe the moisture from your saxophone and put it away safely in its case when you have finished playing.

Quiz time

Dynamic dilemma

ff ***mp*** ***pp*** ***p*** ***mf*** ***f***

Can you put the dynamics in the correct order going from the softest to the loudest?

Softest							Loudest

The high life

Draw a circle around the higher note in each of these pairs (if you're not sure play them both on your saxophone and listen to the sounds to help you decide which one's higher).

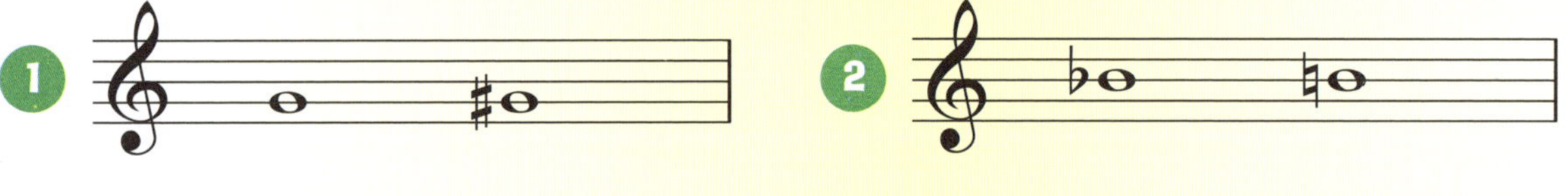

Long to short

Put these notes in the correct order from the longest to the shortest then write underneath each one how many beats it is worth. The first one has been done for you.

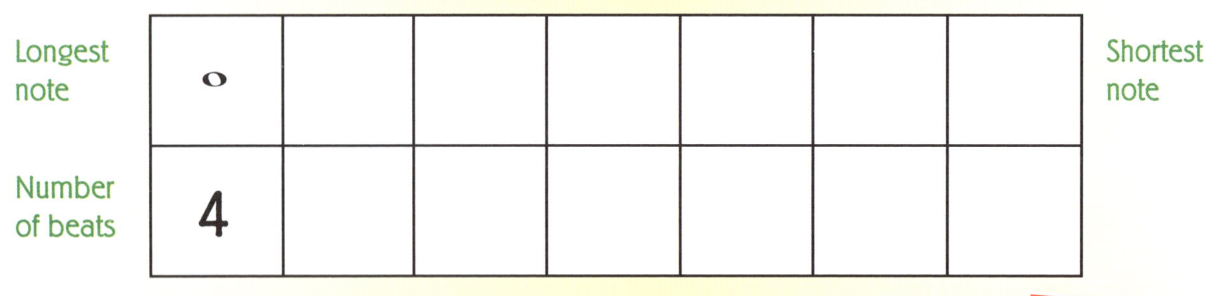

Longest note	𝅝							Shortest note
Number of beats	4							

Now try these pieces from Super Sax Repertoire Book 2

Morning has broken p.32
Swim with dolphins p.34

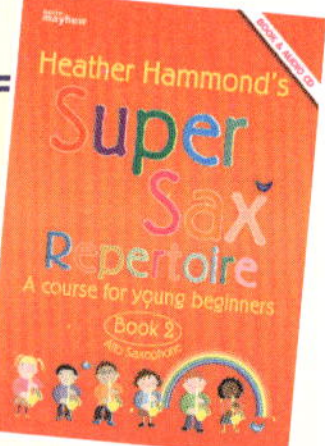

SET 7 A new rhythm

This is a dotted quaver. It is worth 3/4 of a beat.

A dotted quaver can be grouped with a semiquaver to equal 1 beat.

This is a dotted quaver rest – you have to be silent for 3/4 of a beat.

This is a semiquaver rest – you have to be silent for 1/4 of a beat.

Practise clapping each of these rhythms four times.
Then clap the whole thing through twice with the CD accompaniment.

1

2

3

4

MORE OCTAVE HOPS

Here are two E flats

This is how you play
low E flat (E)

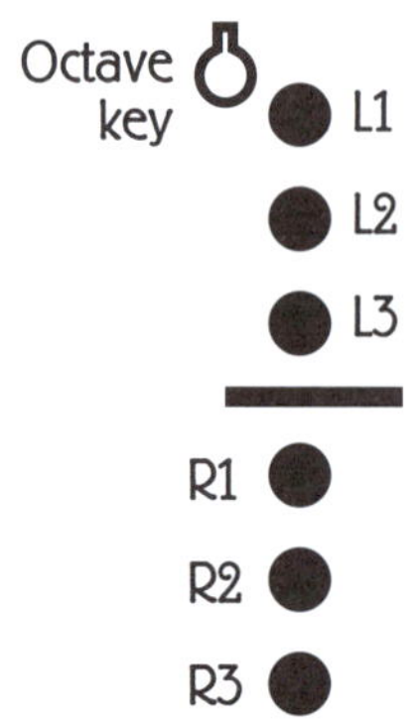

This is what
low E flat (E♭)
looks like on the stave

As you've probably already guessed, just add the octave key to get the high E♭.

This is how you play
high E flat (E♭)

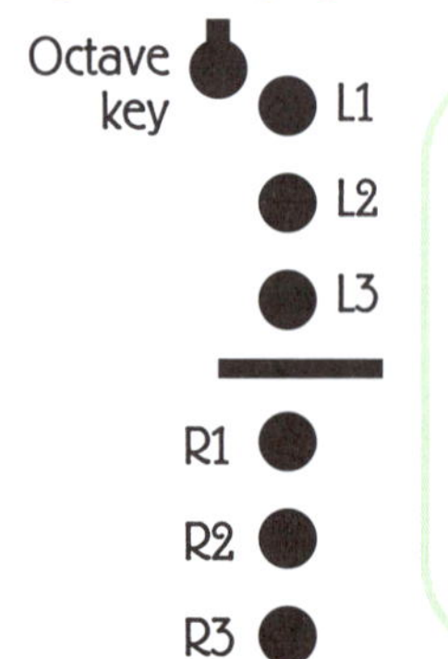

This is what
high E flat (E♭)
looks like on the stave

Know the notes

Practise each of these patterns four times.

1

2

Another enharmonic – E♭ could also be called D♯.

3

4

This key signature tells us to play both B flats and E flats.

Choc-chip Charlie

Jolly moderato

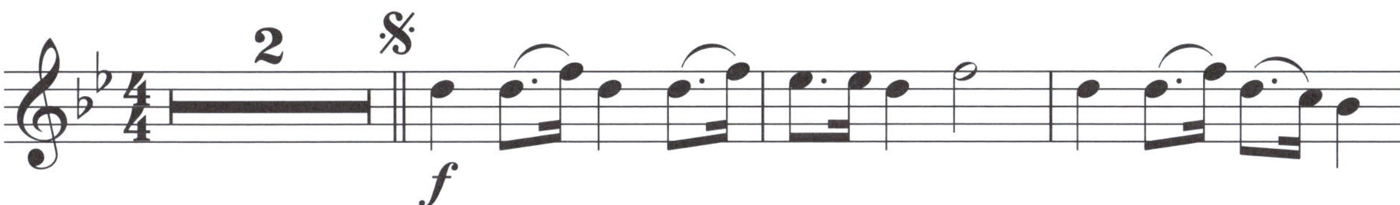

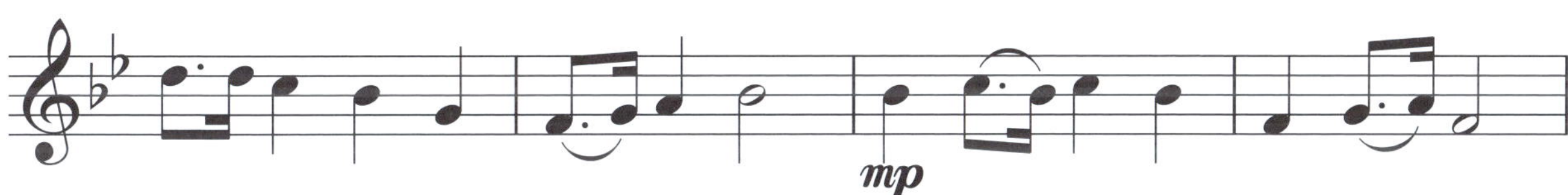

Before you start playing a piece always check the structure.
Look out for any repeat signs ||: :||, returns to the beginning (D.C.), returns to the 𝄋 sign (D.S.) and if there's a coda 𝄌 at the end, how do you get there?

E harmonic minor scale

Watch out for the F♯ in the key signature. There's also a D♯ but that appears beside the note as an accidental (so you are less likely to forget that one!).

Silly Millie

With a steady, bouncy beat

Using the notes below and the rhythm ♩. ♪, listen to the CD and try to copy the tunes like an echo. The first one starts on F.

Remember not to worry if you don't get them all right first time!

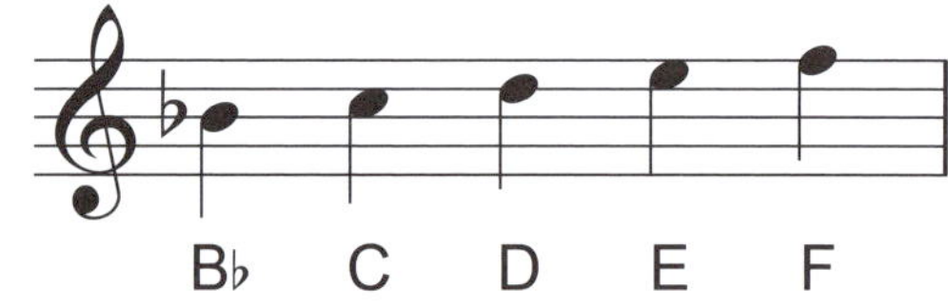

Now try this piece from Super Sax Repertoire Book 2 — Country gardens p.36

Sounds familiar?

Can you add the missing items to complete this well-known tune?

1. Put an F sharp and a C sharp in the key signature.
2. Put in a time signature that means 3 crotchet beats in every bar.
3. Add a B crotchet.
4. Add a high D note worth 1 beat.
5. Add a high C sharp minim.
6. Add a low A semiquaver.
7. Add a bar line.
8. Add a 1 beat note using the highest A that you know so far.
9. Add a dotted quaver using the highest G that you know so far.
10. Add the highest F sharp that you know as a crotchet.
11. Add the highest E that you know as a crotchet.
12. Add a double bar line at the end of the music.
13. Now play the tune.
14. Add the title above the tune.

Song title:

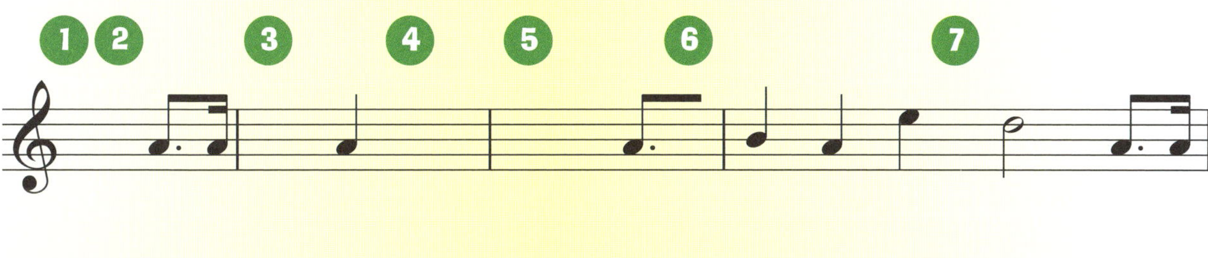

SET 8 A new time signature – $\frac{6}{8}$

In $\frac{6}{8}$ time there are 6 quavers in each bar. The quavers are grouped in threes.

The first quaver has a strong accent but the fourth quaver needs a slight stress too, like this.

You usually count two ♩. beats per bar in $\frac{6}{8}$ time.

Practise clapping each of these rhythms four times.
Then clap the whole thing through twice with the CD accompaniment.

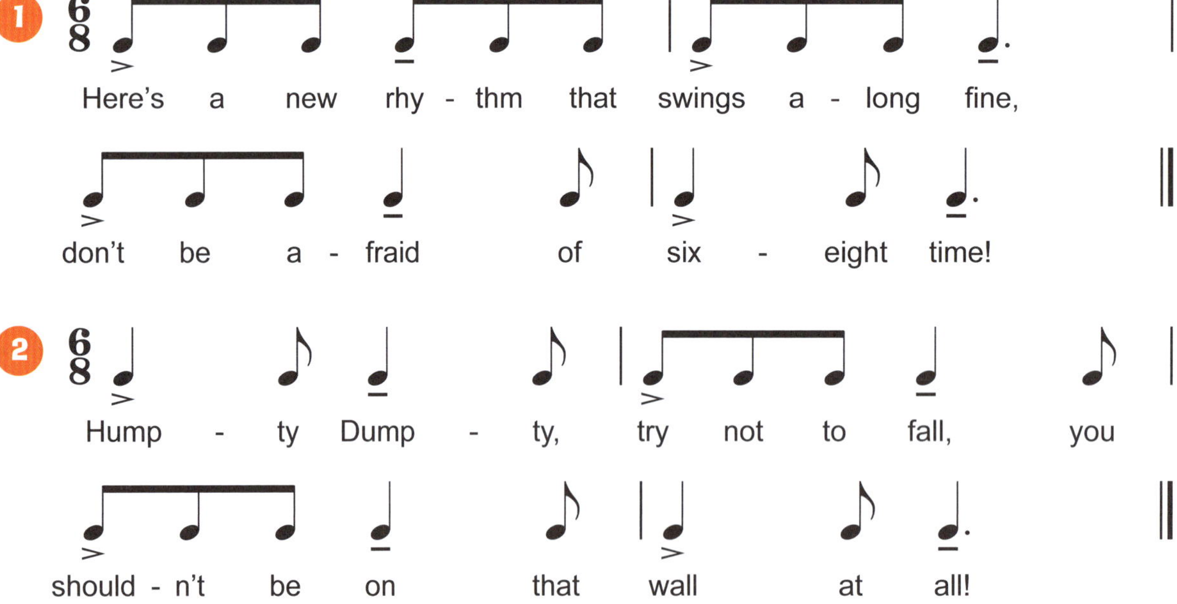

Arpeggios are formed from the 1st, 3rd and 5th notes of scales.

Arpeggio of F major

Arpeggio of G major

Notice that rests can be dotted just like notes.

The dotted crotchet rest is worth 1 ½ crotchet beats (or in this case, where we are counting ♩. beats, it is worth 1 beat).

Jim-jam jig

TRACK 44 COMPLETE
TRACK 45 BACKING

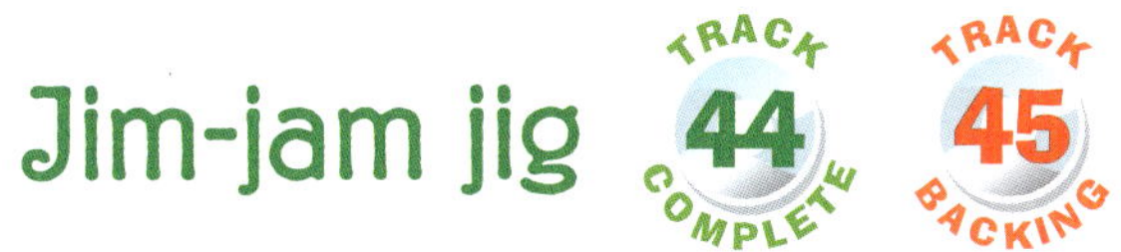

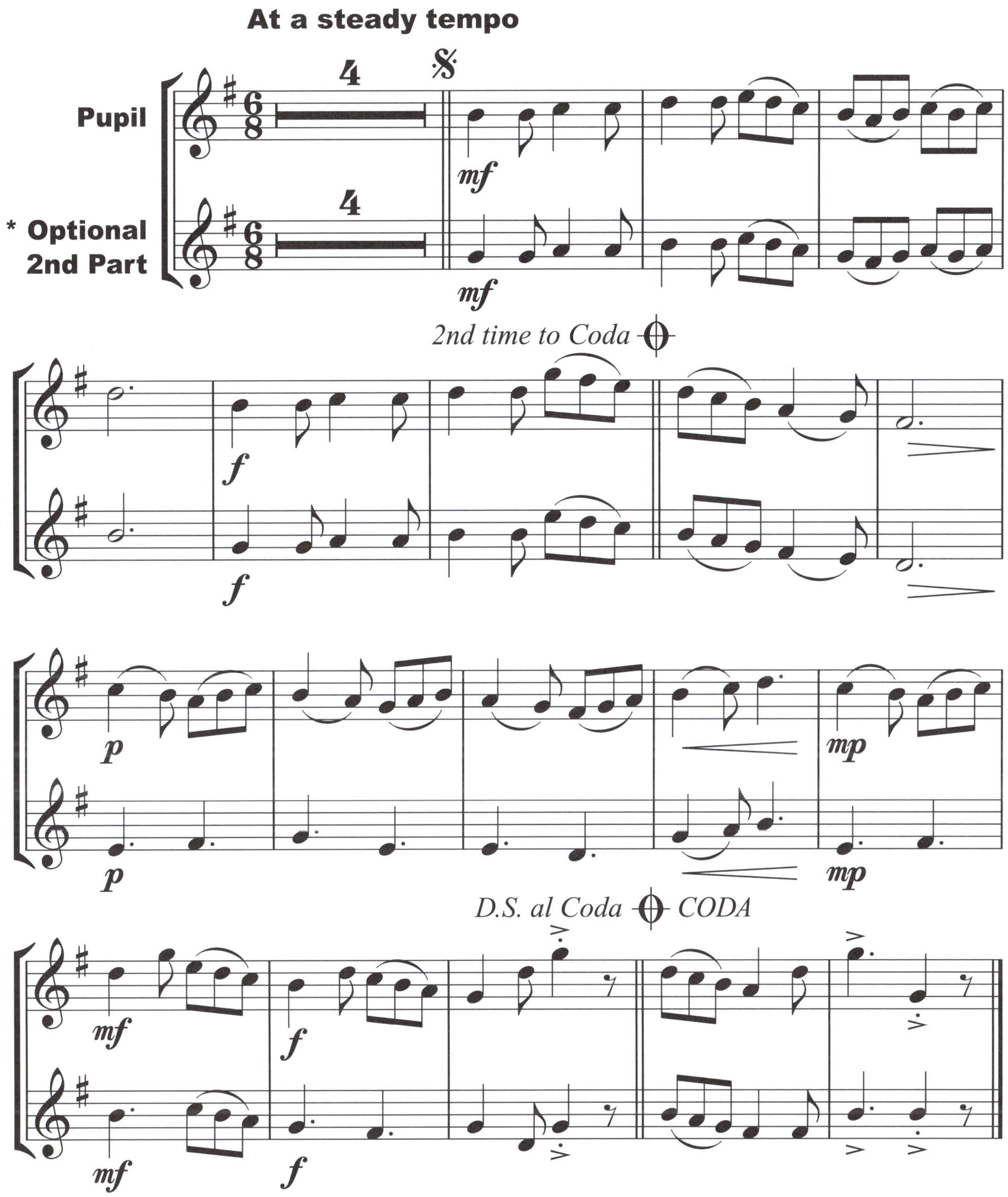
At a steady tempo
Pupil
* Optional 2nd Part
4
4
mf
mf
2nd time to Coda
f
f
p
p
mp
mp
D.S. al Coda
CODA
mf
f
mf
f

* *Optional 2nd part for your teacher or a friend*

Don't forget that it's best to practise fast pieces slowly at first.
Gradually speed them up as you become more familiar with the notes.

Arpeggio of A minor

Arpeggio of E minor

Reminders

There are some tempo changes in the following piece.

rit.	held back (suddenly slower)
rall.	becoming gradually slower
a tempo	back to the original speed

For Av and Laine

Moonlight reflections

TRACK 46 COMPLETE

TRACK 47 BACKING

Adagio

4

mp

poco rit.

a tempo

mf

poco rit. *a tempo*

f *p*

mf

rit. *a tempo*

f *mp*

rall.

Crossword fun

First see how many answers you know without looking them up. For the ones you're not sure about the answers can all be found earlier in this book.

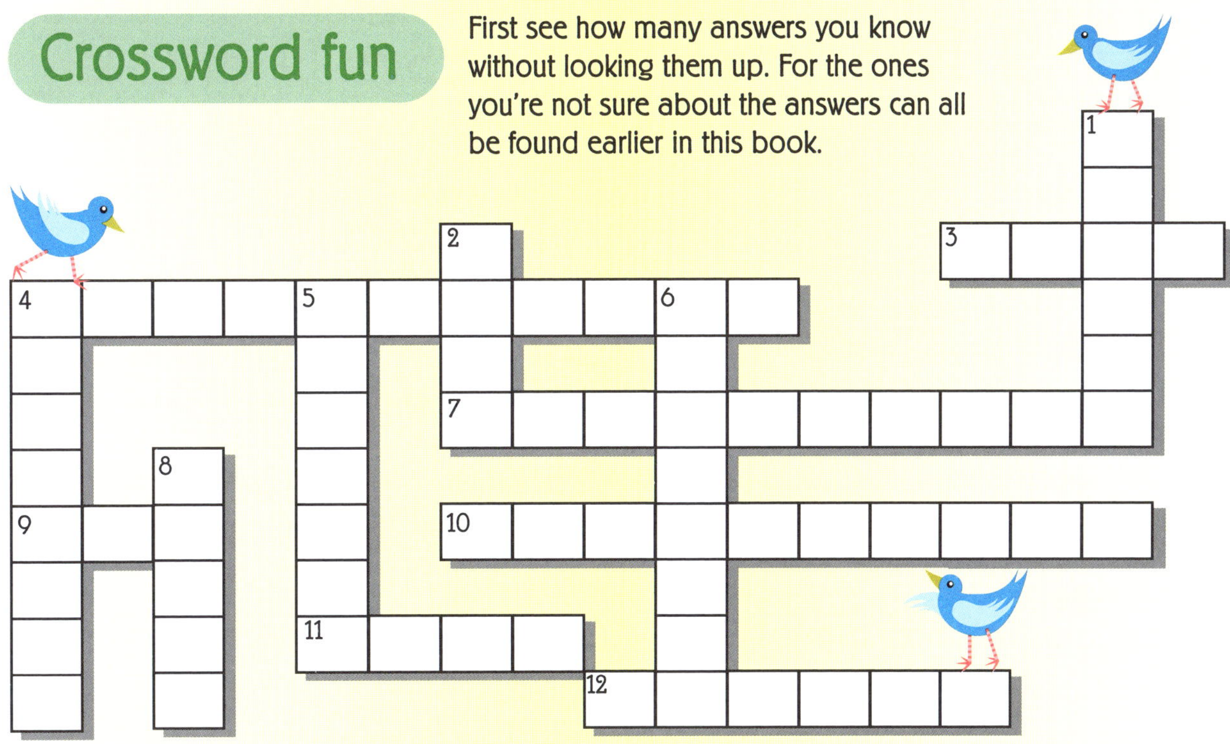

Clues

1. An Italian word for slow.

2. How many beats is this rest worth if you are in $\frac{4}{4}$ time? 𝄾

3. The name for this sign. ♭

4 across. Four of these notes are played in the time of one crotchet.

4 down. The distance between A and A flat for example.

5. There are six of these in every bar in $\frac{6}{8}$ time.

6. The full Italian word meaning held back (suddenly slower).

7. An Italian word telling you to play very loudly.

8. The Italian word for movement.

9. For how many crotchet beats should you rest if you see this sign? 𝄼

10. The Italian word telling you to play very softly.

11. The name of the sign that tells you to play smoothly.

12. $\frac{4}{4}$ time can also be called _ _ _ _ _ _ time.

Now try these pieces from Super Sax Repertoire Book 2

If Alice feels blue p.38
Greensleeves p.40
Ballade pour Louise p.42

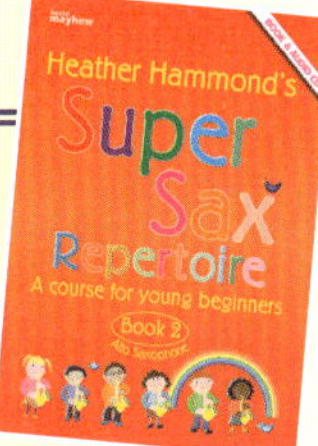

SET 9 Two new low notes – D and C

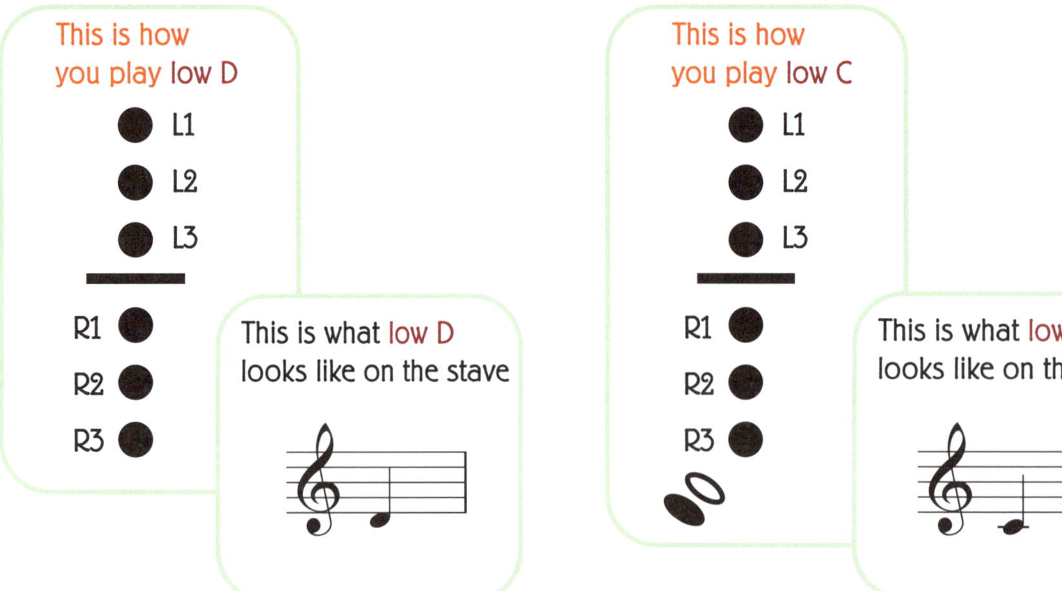

It can be quite difficult to make a good sound when you're playing the low notes at first.
Try to relax, play with an open throat (see Book 1, page 8)
and make sure that you're providing a good supply of air.
Try not to sound like a fog horn!

Know the notes

Practise each of these patterns four times.

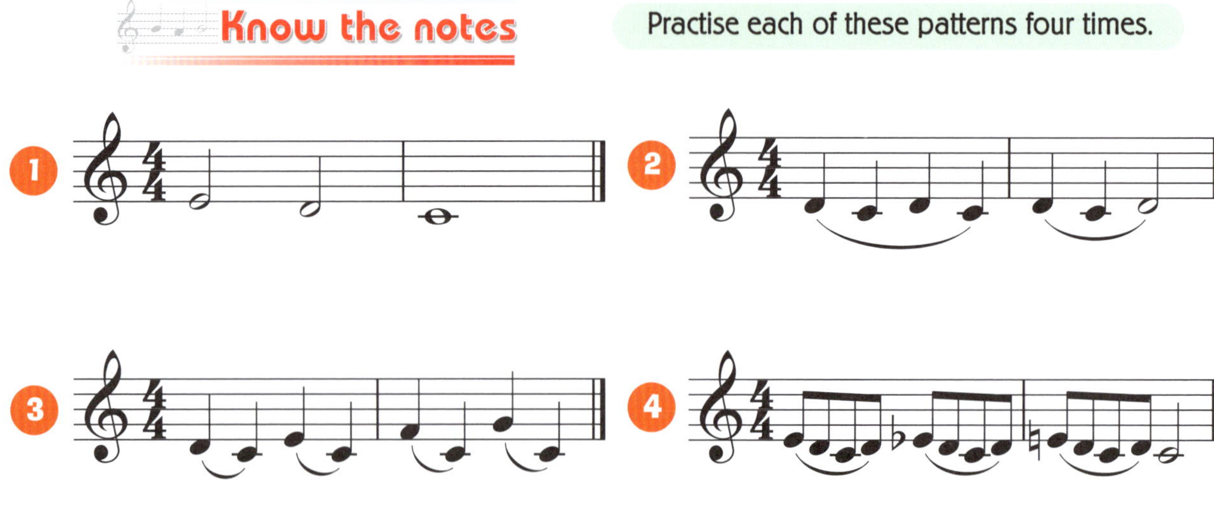

Long note practice 3

TRACK 48

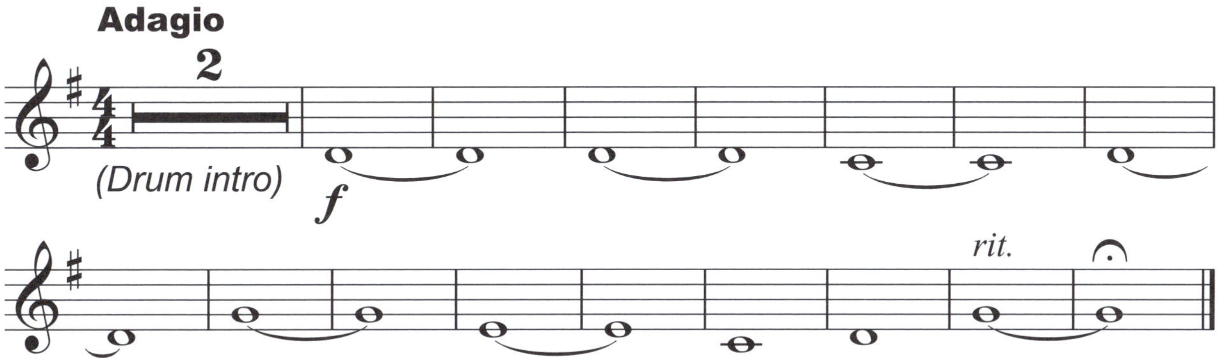

Adagio
2
(Drum intro)
f
rit.

Rock 'n' roll road

TRACK 49 COMPLETE

TRACK 50 BACKING

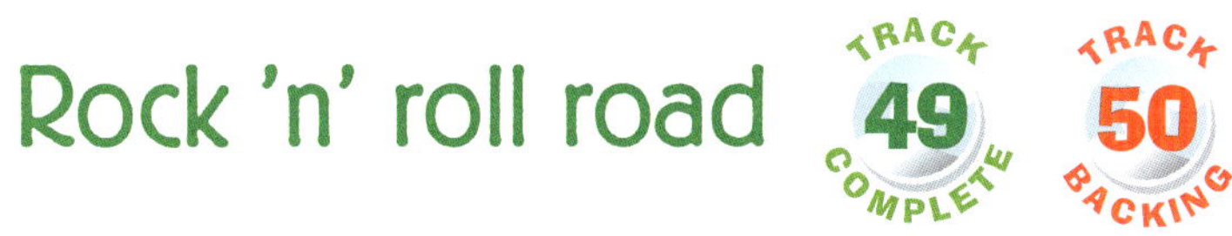

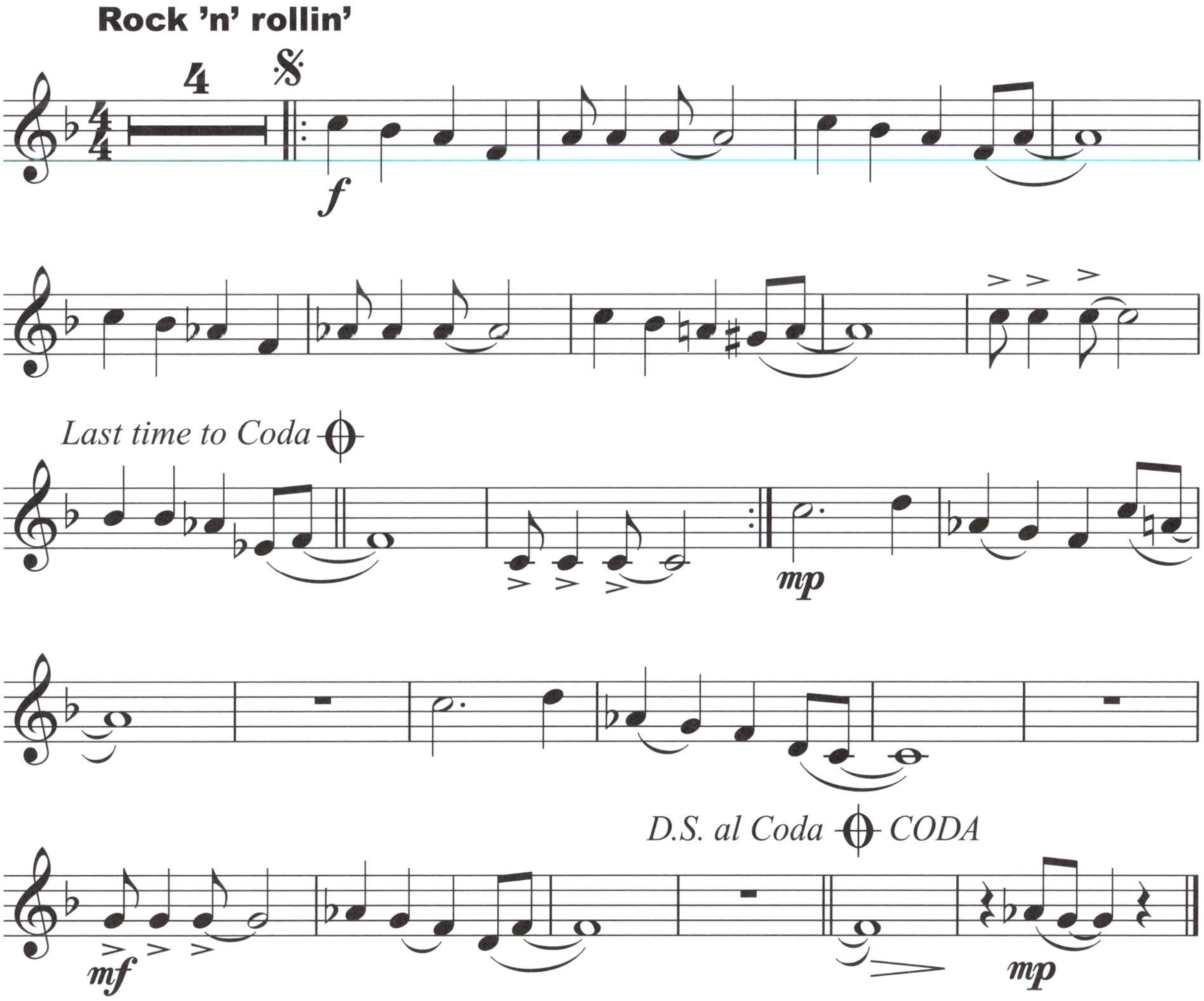
Rock 'n' rollin'
4
f
Last time to Coda
mp
D.S. al Coda
CODA
mf
mp

Listen to the CD and try to copy the tunes.

Hint: They all start on D. Each one will use either F or F♯ (but never both). If you think the tune sounds sad or bluesy then it will be an F, if it's a jolly, happy tune then it will be an F♯.

Using these notes

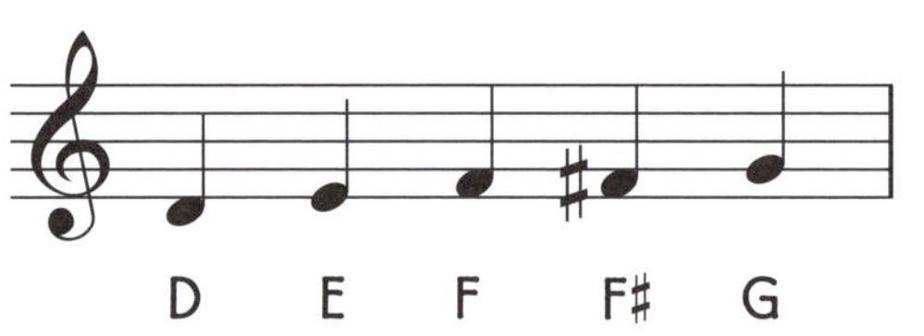

Swinging the quavers

In jazz music you often play quavers in a different way.
So far you have just played 'straight' quavers.

To 'swing' the quavers you make the first one longer than it normally would be – it is allowed to take up $^2/_3$ of the crotchet beat instead of $^1/_2$.

The second quaver then has to become shorter than it would usually be – it lasts for just $^1/_3$ of a crotchet beat.

Here's the maths

Straight Quavers

Swing Quavers

Beats 1 $^1/_2$ $^1/_2$ $^1/_2$ $^1/_2$ $^1/_2$ $^1/_2$

1 $^2/_3$ $^1/_3$ $^2/_3$ $^1/_3$ $^2/_3$ $^1/_3$

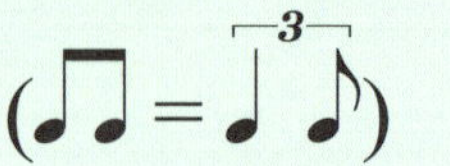

This sign at the beginning of a piece tells you to swing the quavers. Sometimes it will just say 'swing'.

Straight Swing

Listen to the first track and then compare the quavers to the second when they are swung to get the feel of the swung quavers. It's not as complicated as the maths looks! Practise clapping each of these rhythms four times first with straight quavers, then with swung quavers. Listen to the drums – they will help you to get the correct feel for your quavers each time.

Always play something for fun in each session. You could try an easy piece that you have never seen before (this is called sight-reading) or play some of your old favourite pieces that you learnt in the past.

Now here's a piece for you to try out your swing-quaver playing.

Steam train swing

TRACK 54 COMPLETE

TRACK 55 BACKING

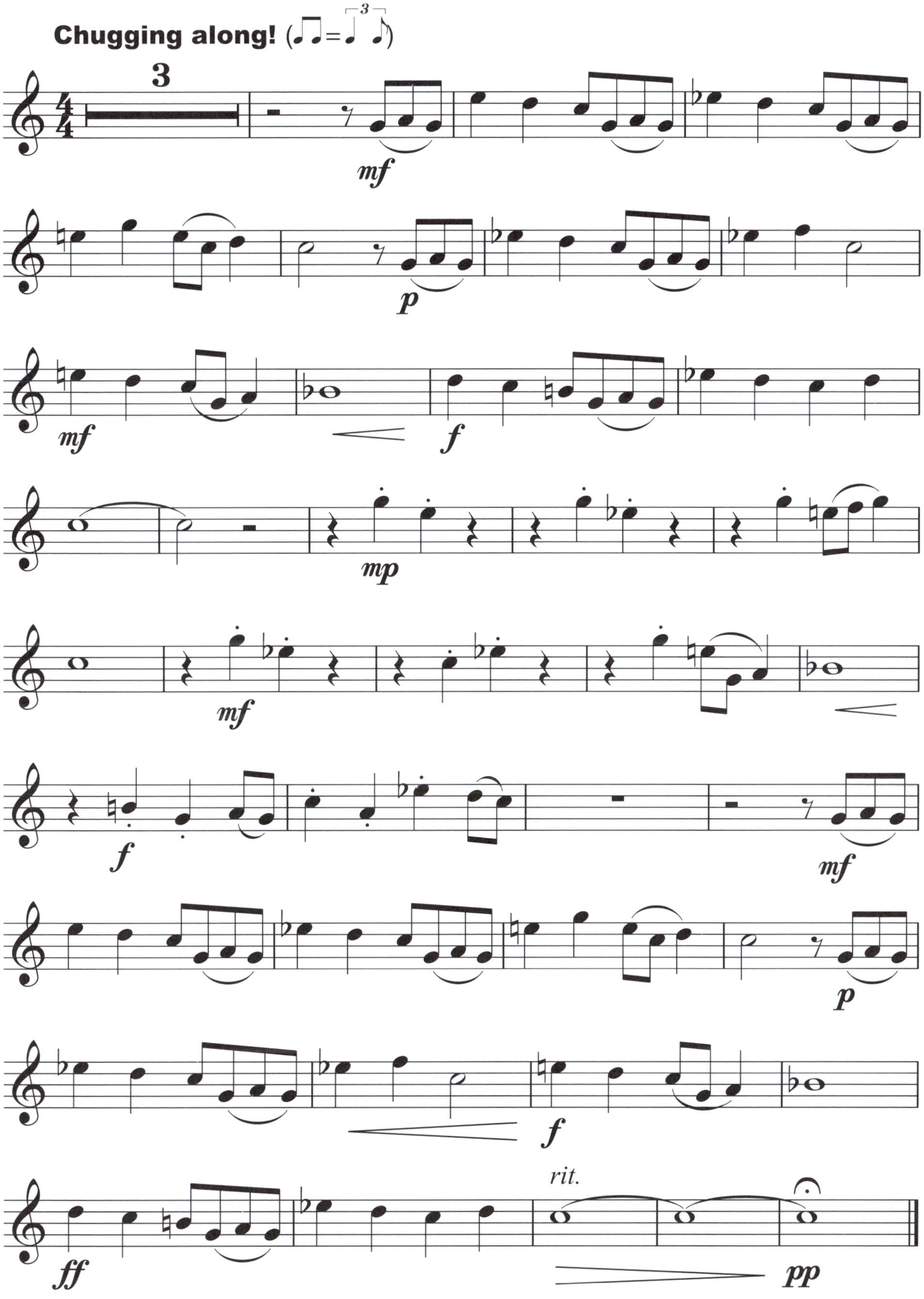
Chugging along!
rit.

The next tune uses the key signature that tells us to play both F sharps and C sharps. Also watch out for the A sharp that appears at the beginning of the 1st and 2nd time bars (remember A♯ = B♭). Don't forget to swing the quavers.

Lotta bother blues

Laid back and very bluesy (♪♪ = ♩ ♪ triplet)

4

p

mp

mf

1.

mp

2.

rit.

pp

Now try these pieces from Super Sax Repertoire Book 2

Just another love song p.45
Half a world away p.48
Funk factory p.50

D harmonic minor scale

D minor arpeggio

Enharmonic Quiz (same note – different name)

Can you find another name for each of the following notes? The first one has been done for you.

1 C♯ = D♭

2 .... = ...

3 .... = ...

4 .... = ...

5 .... = ...

6 .... = ...

7 .... = ...

8 .... = ...

SET 10 And finally – low C sharp

This is what low C sharp (C♯) looks like on the stave

This is how you play low C sharp (C♯)

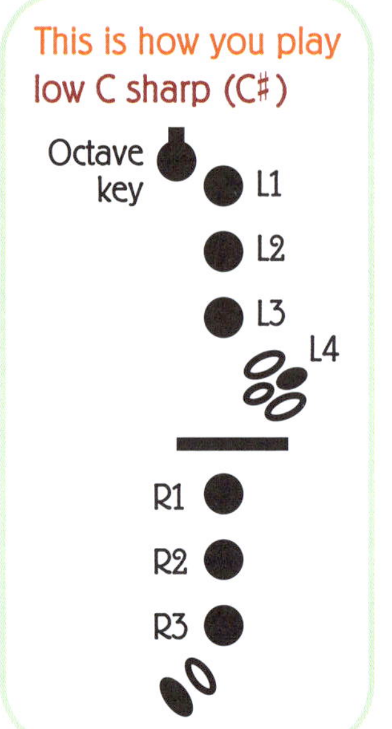

Know the notes

Practise each of these patterns four times.

1 

2 

3 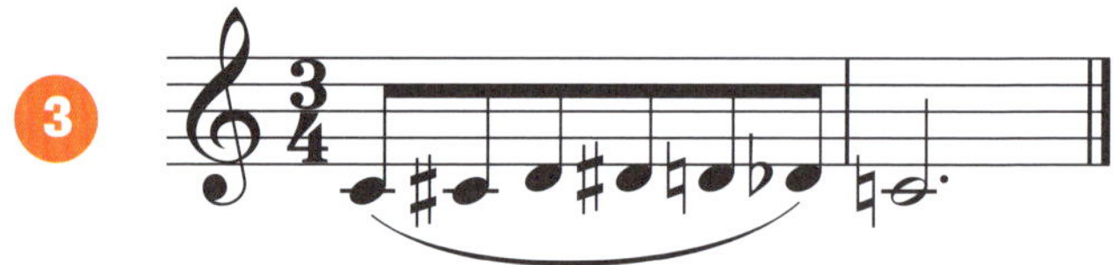

4 

You may find it helpful to play low notes fairly loudly at first.

D major scale

Remember to check the key signature before you start to play.

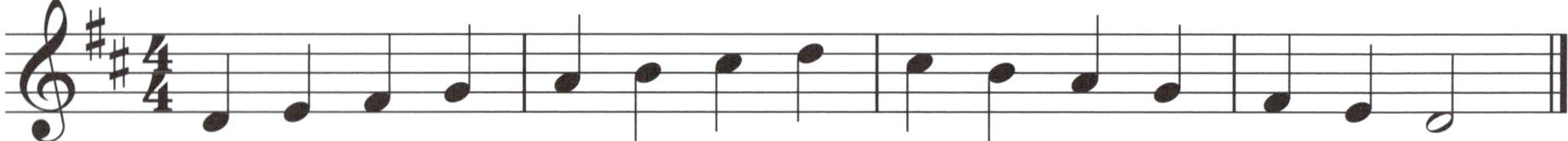

D major arpeggio

Always warm up at the start of your practice with some exercises, long note playing or scales and arpeggios before moving on to your pieces.

Here's a piece to practise your low note playing.

Don't forget (♫ = ♩ ♪) means that you swing the quavers.

Simon says 'Swing it'

TRACK 58 COMPLETE

TRACK 59 BACKING

Laid-back swing style (♫ = ♩ ♪)

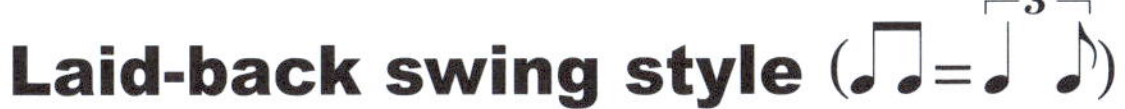

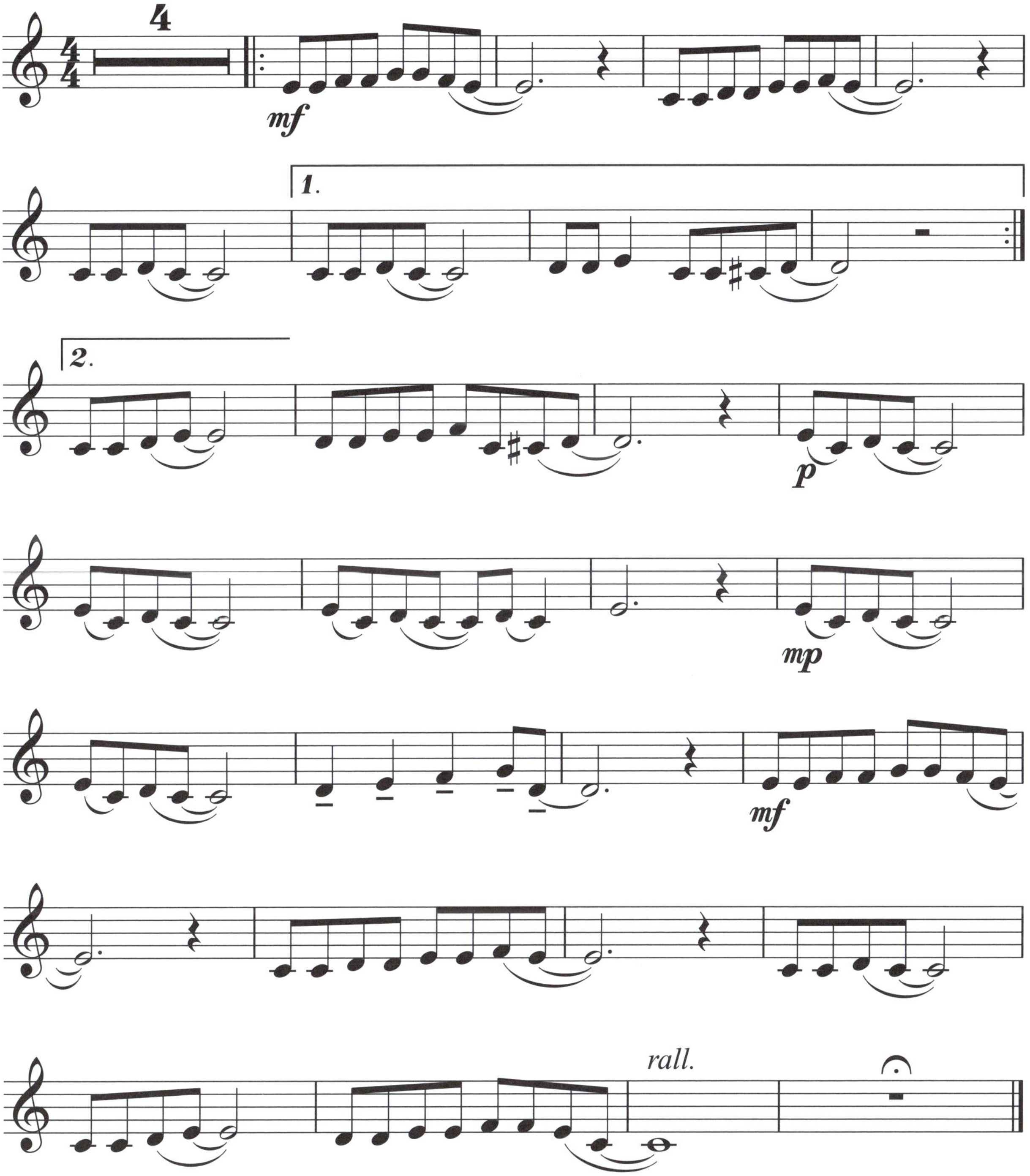

Now here's exactly the same tune again (apart from an extra note at the end!).
This time though, play with a rock feel (do not swing the quavers). Which version do you prefer?

Simon says 'Rock it'

When you know a few pieces really well, why not give a concert to your friends or family? Playing to an audience is a great way of helping you to become a real performer.

Quiz time

Decide which is the correct answer to each of the questions and place the corresponding letter in the answer box provided. If you answer all the questions accurately the name of a musical instrument will appear reading downwards.

						Answer letter
		P	T	C	D	
1. (dotted crotchet rest)	How many quavers is this worth?	1	2	3	4	
		R	A	N	L	
2.	G♯ is exactly the same as:-	B♭	G	F♯	A♭	
		E	U	A	O	
3.	'poco rall.' means	a little higher	a little faster	a little slower	a little softer	
		P	R	M	S	
4. (treble clef, two flats)	Which notes will be played as flats?	A♭ and B♭	B♭ and E♭	B♭ and D♭	A♭ and E♭	
		I	B	P	D	
5.	The sign for a coda is	𝄌	𝄾	𝄋	♮	
		N	O	E	R	
6. (treble clef, one sharp)	Which major scale uses this key signature?	G	C	D	F	
		S	T	E	N	
7.	In $\frac{6}{8}$ time how many dotted crotchet beats should be counted in each bar?	1	3	2	4	
		D	T	E	N	
8. (:‖)	What does this sign mean?	Go to the coda	Repeat	Common time	Stop playing	

The musical instrument is a _ _ _ _ _ _ _ _

Now try these pieces from Super Sax Repertoire Book 2

Jazzin' at the tree house p.52
Portsmouth p.54

Notes

This is to certify that

___

has successfully completed

Super Sax Book 2

and is now promoted to

Super Sax Book 3

___

Teacher

___

Date

WELL DONE!